PIANO • VOCAL • GUITAR

THE GRAMMY AWARDS®

RECORD OF THE YEAR
1958 – 2011

Visit The Recording Academy Online at
www.grammy.com

ISBN 978-1-4584-1563-9

7777 W. BLUEMOUND RD. P.O. BOX 13819 MILWAUKEE, WI 53213

Visit Hal Leonard Online at
www.halleonard.com

≫ Adele at the 54th GRAMMY Awards

THE RECORDING ACADEMY®

When it comes to music on TV, the last few years alone have seen some very memorable moments: Paul McCartney, Bruce Springsteen, Dave Grohl, and Joe Walsh jamming on "The End" from the Beatles' classic *Abbey Road*; Adele making her triumphant first live singing appearance after throat surgery to perform "Rolling In The Deep"; Pink dripping wet and hovering 20 feet above the stage while singing a note-perfect version of "Glitter In The Air"; and Lady Gaga hatching from a massive egg to perform "Born This Way." All of these performances, and many more, took place on the famed GRAMMY Awards® stage.

The GRAMMY® Award is indisputedly the most coveted recognition of excellence in recorded music worldwide. Over more than half a century, the GRAMMY Awards have become both music's biggest honor and Music's Biggest Night®, with the annual telecast drawing tens of millions of viewers nationwide and millions more internationally.

And with evolving categories that always reflect important current artistic waves — such as dance/electronica music — as well as setting a record for social TV engagement in 2012, the GRAMMYs keep moving forward, serving as a real-time barometer of music's cultural impact.

The Recording Academy is the organization that produces the GRAMMY Awards. Consisting of the artists, musicians, songwriters, producers, engineers, and other professionals who make the music you enjoy every day on the radio, your streaming or download services, or in the concert hall, The Academy is a dynamic institution with an active agenda aimed at supporting and nurturing music and the people who make it.

Whether it's joining with recording artists to ensure their creative rights are protected, providing ongoing professional development services to the recording community or supporting the health and well-being of music creators and music education in our schools, The Recording Academy has become the recording industry's primary organization for professional and educational outreach, human services, arts advocacy, and cultural enrichment.

The Academy represents members from all corners of the professional music world — from the biggest recording stars to unsung music educators — all brought together under the banner of building a better creative environment for music and its makers.

» Paul McCartney at the 2012 MusiCares Person of the Year gala in his honor

» Trombone Shorty and Mavis Staples at the GRAMMY Foundation's Music Preservation Project event in 2012

MUSICARES FOUNDATION®

MusiCares® was established by The Recording Academy to provide a safety net of critical assistance for music people in times of need. MusiCares has developed into a premier support system for music people, providing resources to cover a wide range of financial, medical and personal emergencies through innovative programs and services, including regular eBay auctions of one-of-a-kind memorabilia that are open to the public. The charity has been supported by the contributions and participation of artists such as Neil Diamond, Aretha Franklin, Paul McCartney, Bruce Springsteen, Barbra Streisand, and Neil Young — just to name the organization's most recent annual Person of the Year fundraiser honorees — and so many others through the years.

THE GRAMMY FOUNDATION®

The GRAMMY Foundation's mission is to cultivate the understanding, appreciation and advancement of the contribution of recorded music to American culture. The Foundation accomplishes this mission through programs and activities designed to engage the music industry and cultural community as well as the general public. The Foundation works to bring national attention to important issues such as the value and impact of music and arts education and the urgency of preserving our rich cultural legacy, and it accomplishes this work by engaging music professionals — from big-name stars to working professionals and educators — to work directly with students.

» Secretary of the Department of Health and Human Services Kathleen Sebelius and Recording Academy President/CEO Neil Portnow present the Recording Artists' Coalition Award to John Mayer at the GRAMMYs on the Hill Awards in Washington, D.C. in 2012

Paul Morigi/WireImage.com

GRAMMY MUSEUM

PIERRE COSSETTE CENTER

» The GRAMMY Museum in downtown Los Angeles

Courtesy of the GRAMMY Museum

FIGHTING FOR MUSICIANS' RIGHTS

Over the last 15 years, The Recording Academy has built a presence in the nation's capital, working to amplify the voice of music creators in national policy matters. Today, called the "supersized musicians lobby" by *Congressional Quarterly*, The Academy's Advocacy & Industry Relations office in Washington, D.C., is the leading representative of the collective world of recording professionals — artists, songwriters, producers, and engineers — through its GRAMMYs on the Hill® Initiative. The Academy has taken a leadership role in the fight to expand radio performance royalties to all music creators, worked on behalf of musicians on censorship concerns and regularly supported musicians on legislative issues that impact the vitality of music.

THE GRAMMY MUSEUM®

Since opening its doors in December 2008, the GRAMMY Museum has served as a dynamic educational and interactive institution dedicated to the power of music. The four-story, 30,000-square foot facility is part of L.A. Live, the premier sports and entertainment destination in downtown Los Angeles. The Museum serves the community with interactive, permanent and traveling exhibits and an array of public and education programs. We invite you to visit us when you're in the Los Angeles area.

As you can see, The Recording Academy is so much more than the annual GRAMMY telecast once a year, even if that one show is Music's Biggest Night. To keep up with all The Academy's activities, visit GRAMMY.com regularly, and join the conversation on our social networks:

 Facebook.com/TheGRAMMYs

 Twitter.com/TheGRAMMYs

 YouTube.com/TheGRAMMYs

 TheGRAMMYs.tumblr.com

 Foursquare.com/TheGRAMMYs

 Instagram (user name: TheGRAMMYs)

 Google+ (gplus.to/TheGRAMMYs)

TABLE OF CONTENTS (ALPHABETICAL)

TABLE OF CONTENTS (CHRONOLOGICAL)

ALL I WANNA DO

Words and Music by KEVIN GILBERT,
DAVID BAERWALD, SHERYL CROW,
WYN COOPER and BILL BOTTRELL

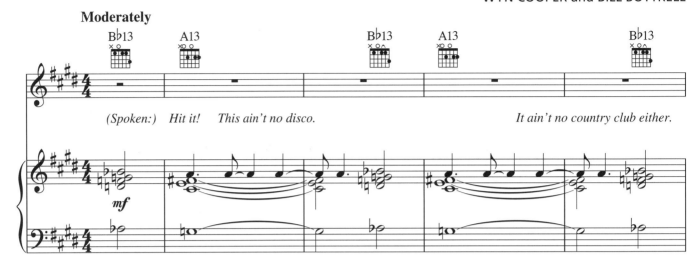

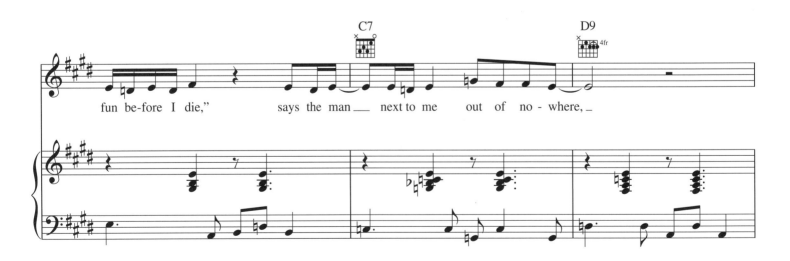

14

(Vocal 1st time only)

Additional Lyrics

3. I like a good beer buzz early in the morning,
   And Billy likes to peel the labels from his bottles of Bud
   And shred them on the bar.
   Then he lights every match in an oversized pack,
   Letting each one burn down to his thick fingers
   Before blowing and cursing them out.
   And he's watching the Buds as they spin on the floor.
   A happy couple enters the bar dancing dangerously close to one another.
   The bartender looks up from his want ads.
   Chorus

ANOTHER DAY IN PARADISE

Words and Music by
PHIL COLLINS

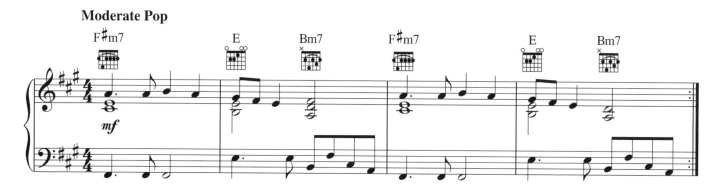

She calls out __ to the man __ on the street, __ "Sir, __ can you help __
He walks on, __ does - n't look back. __ He pre - tends __ he can't hear __
She calls out __ to the man __ on the street. __ He can see __ she's been cry -
You can tell __ from the lines __ on her face. __ You can see __ that she's been __

__ me? It's cold __ and I've no - where to sleep.
__ her. Starts to whis - tle as he cross - es the street.
- ing. She's got blis - ters on the soles __ of her feet. __
__ there. Prob - a - bly been moved on from ev - er - y place __

22

AQUARIUS/LET THE SUNSHINE IN

from the Broadway Musical Production HAIR

Words by JAMES RADO and GEROME RAGNI
Music by GALT MacDERMOT

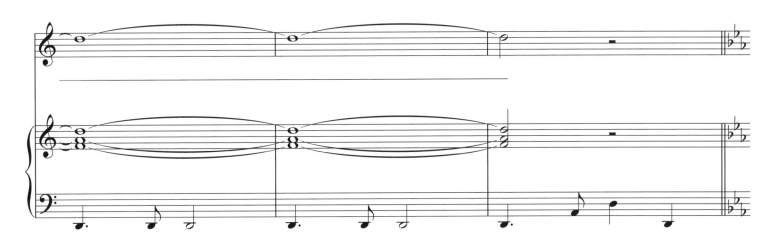

Moderately slow Rock, with a beat

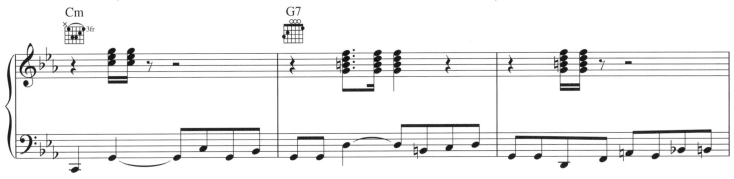

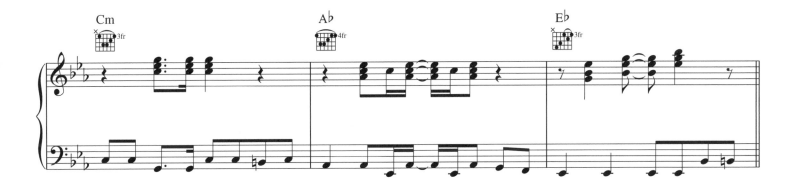

Let ___ the sun ___ shine. ___ Let ___ the sun -

BEAT IT

Words and Music by
MICHAEL JACKSON

They told him, "Don't you ev - er come a - round here. Don't wan - na see your face; you bet - ter
They're out to get you. Bet - ter leave while you can. Don't wan - na be a boy; you wan - na

Instrumental

dis - ap - pear." The fi - re's in their eyes and their words are real - ly clear. So
be a man. You wan - na stay a - live; bet - ter do what you can. So

Original key: E♭ minor. This edition has been transposed up one half-step to be more playable.

BEAUTIFUL DAY

Lyrics by BONO
Music by U2

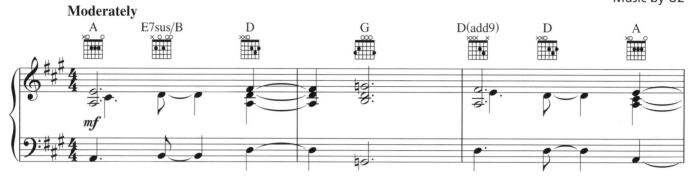

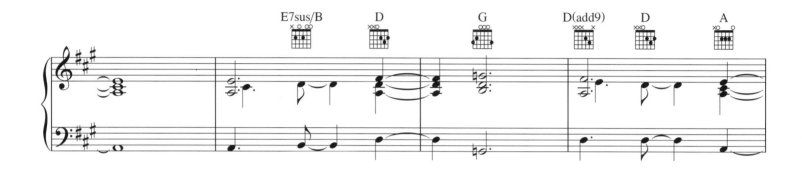

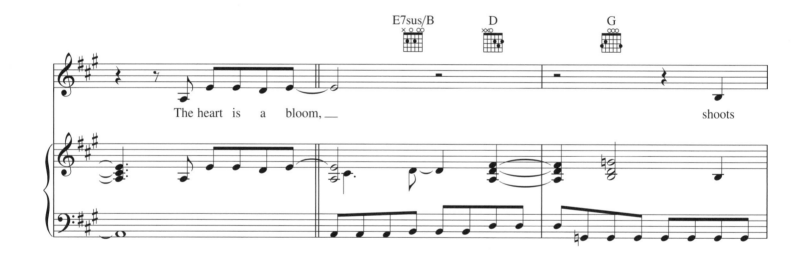

The heart is a bloom, __ shoots

up through the ston- y ground. __ But there's no room, __

40

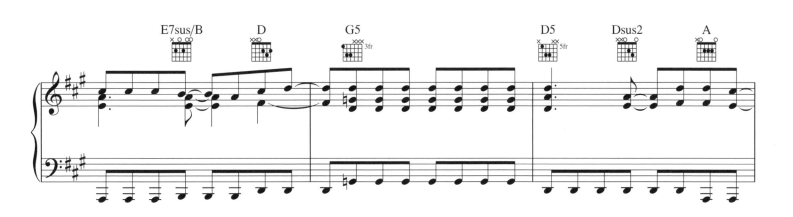

BETTE DAVIS EYES

Words by DONNA WEISS
Music by JACKIE DeSHANNON

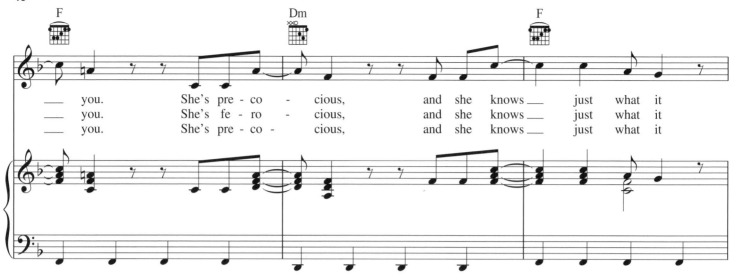

you. She's pre-co - cious, and she knows ___ just what it
you. She's fe-ro - cious, and she knows ___ just what it
you. She's pre-co - cious, and she knows ___ just what it

takes to make ___ a pro ___ blush. She's got Gret - ta Gar - bo
takes to make ___ a pro ___ blush. *All the boys*
takes to make ___ a pro ___ blush. *All the boys*

3rd time **To Coda**

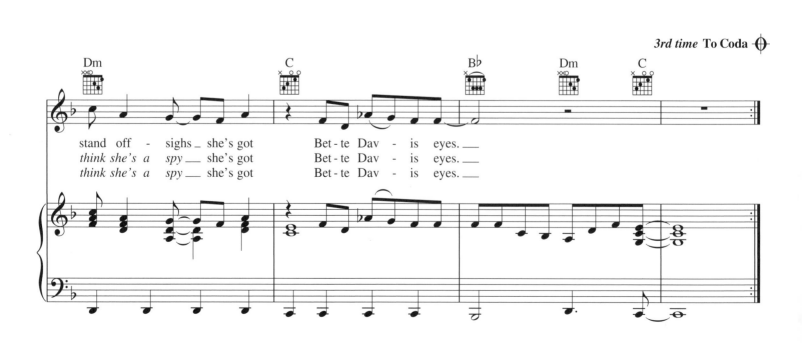

stand off - sighs ___ she's got Bet - te Dav - is eyes. ___
think she's a spy ___ she's got Bet - te Dav - is eyes. ___
think she's a spy ___ she's got Bet - te Dav - is eyes. ___

BOULEVARD OF BROKEN DREAMS

Words by BILLIE JOE ARMSTRONG
Music by GREEN DAY

I walk a lone-ly road, the on-ly one that I ___ have ev-er known. ___
I'm walk-ing down the line that di-vides me ___ some-where in my ___

___ Don't know where it goes, but it's home to me ___ and I walk a-lone. ___
mind. On the bor-der-line of the edge and ___ where I walk a-lone. ___

DON'T WORRY, BE HAPPY

Words and Music by
BOBBY McFERRIN

(Whistle, add higher notes on repeat)

Here's a lit - tle
Ain't got no place to lay
Ain't got no cash, ain't got

song I wrote.___ You might want to sing it note ___ for note.__ Don't
___ your head.___ Some-bod - y came and took ___ your bed.__ Don't
___ no style.___ Ain't got no gal to make ___ you smile.__ Don't

wor - ry, be hap - py.
wor - ry, be hap - py.
wor - ry, be hap - py.

In ev - 'ry life we have ___ some trou - ble,
The land - lord say your rent ___ is late.__
'Cause when you wor - ry your face ___ will frown _

Spoken ad lib. over Repeat and Fade:

Don't worry. Don't worry. Don't do it.
Be happy. Put a smile on your face.
Don't bring everybody down. Don't
worry. It will soon pass, whatever it is.
Don't worry. Be happy. I'm not worried.

I'm happy.

BRIDGE OVER TROUBLED WATER

Words and Music by
PAUL SIMON

Sail on sil - ver girl, sail on

CHANGE THE WORLD

Words and Music by WAYNE KIRKPATRICK,
GORDON KENNEDY and TOMMY SIMS

CLOCKS

Words and Music by GUY BERRYMAN, JON BUCKLAND,
WILL CHAMPION and CHRIS MARTIN

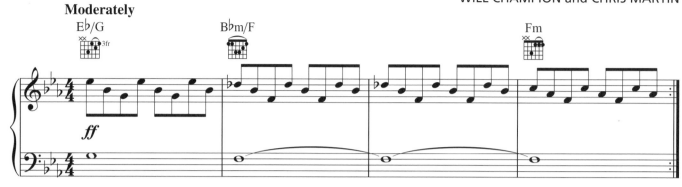

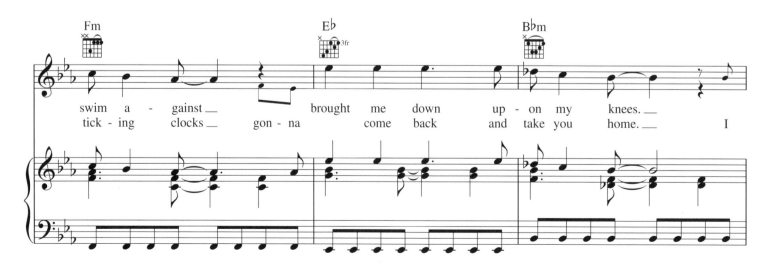

And noth - ing else com - pares. _____

D.S. al Coda
(with repeats)

DAYS OF WINE AND ROSES

Theme from the Film DAYS OF WINE AND ROSES

Lyric by JOHNNY MERCER
Music by HENRY MANCINI

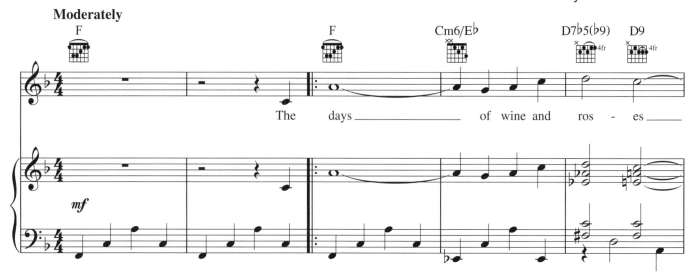

The days _____ of wine and ros - es _____

_____ laugh and run a-way _____ like a child at play, _____ through the

mead-ow-land to-ward a clos-ing door, a door marked "Nev - er - more," that

DON'T KNOW WHY

Words and Music by
JESSE HARRIS

THE FIRST TIME EVER I SAW YOUR FACE

Words and Music by
EWAN MacCOLL

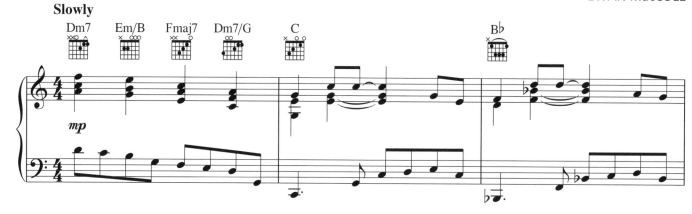

The first __ time _____
The first __ time _____
The first __ time _____

__ ev-er I saw your face,
__ ev-er I kissed your mouth,
__ ev-er I lay with you

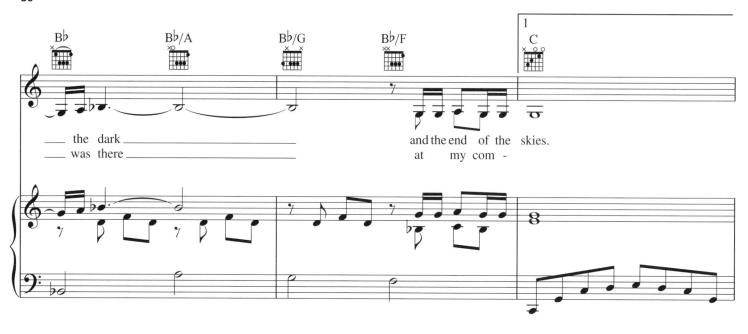

the dark _____ and the end of the skies.
was there _____ at my com -

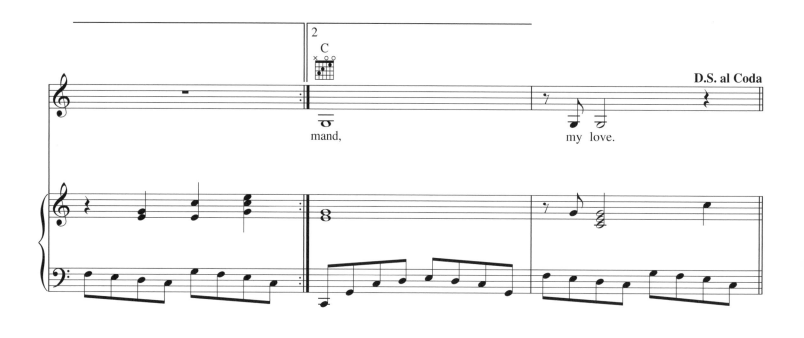

mand, my love.

D.S. al Coda

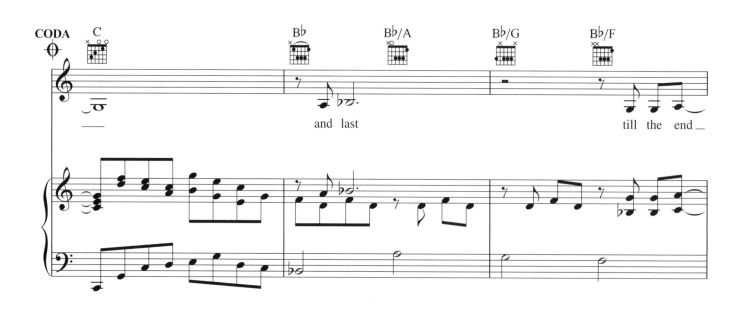

CODA

____ and last till the end ____

THE GIRL FROM IPANEMA
(Garôta de Ipanema)

Music by ANTONIO CARLOS JOBIM
English Words by NORMAN GIMBEL
Original Words by VINICIUS DE MORAES

GRACELAND

Words and Music by
PAUL SIMON

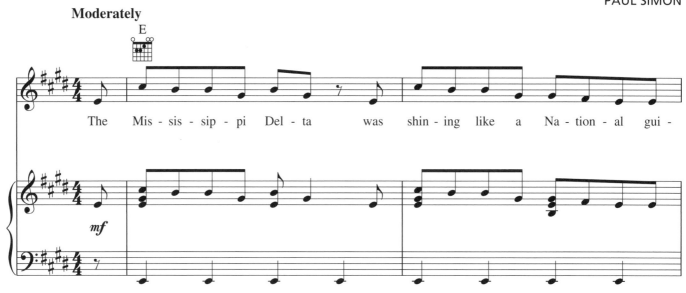

The Mis-sis-sip-pi Del-ta was shin-ing like a Na-tion-al gui-

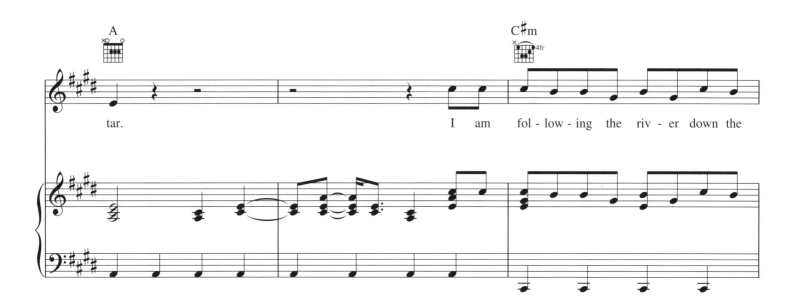

tar. I am fol-low-ing the riv-er down the

high-way through the cra-dle of the Civ-il War.

HERE WE GO AGAIN

Words and Music by
RED STEAGALL and DONNIE LANIER

Cue notes 2nd time

Additional lyrics

3. Here we go again,
   She'll break my heart again, yeah
   I'll play the part again,
   One more time.

HIGHER LOVE

Words and Music by WILL JENNINGS
and STEVE WINWOOD

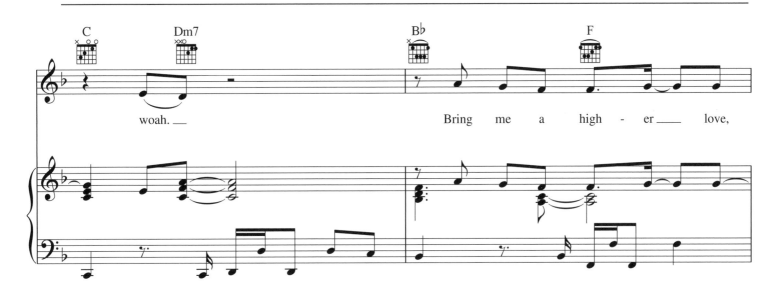

woah. _____ Bring me a high - er _____ love,

bring me a high - er _____ love. _____

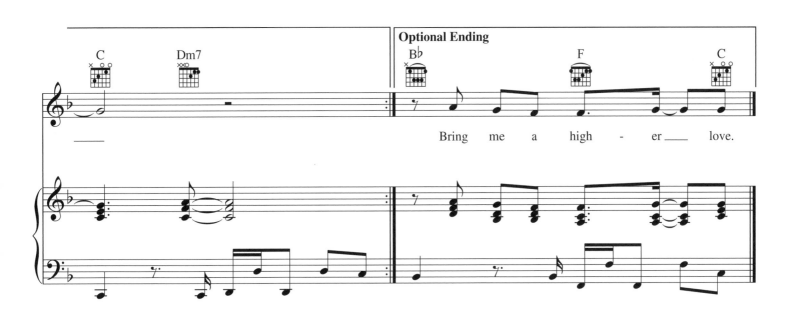

Optional Ending

_____ Bring me a high - er _____ love.

HOTEL CALIFORNIA

Words and Music by DON HENLEY,
GLENN FREY and DON FELDER

Moderate Rock

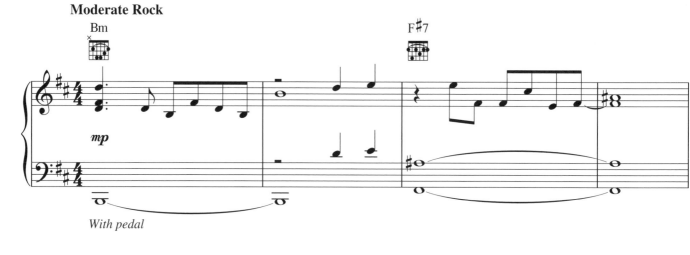

With pedal

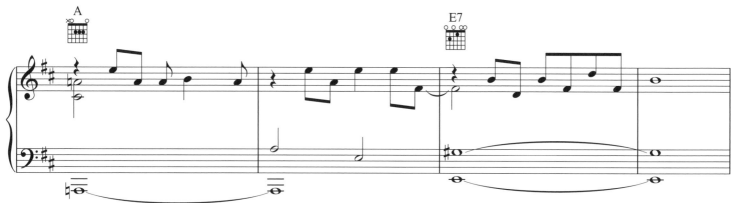

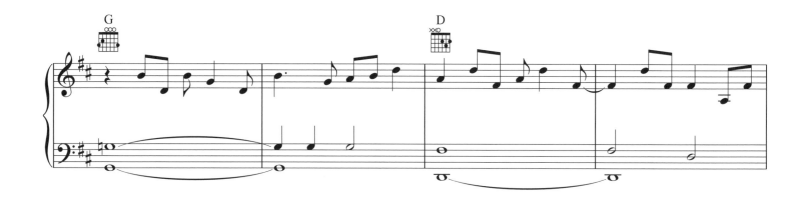

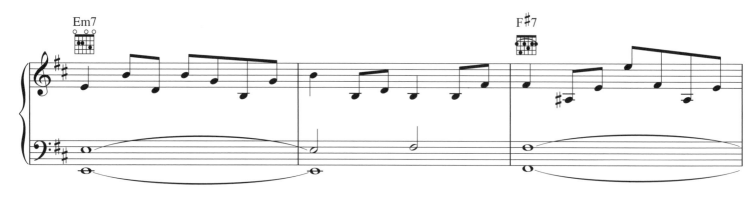

114

I HONESTLY LOVE YOU

Words and Music by JEFF BARRY
and PETER ALLEN

I LEFT MY HEART IN SAN FRANCISCO

Words by DOUGLASS CROSS
Music by GEORGE CORY

I WILL ALWAYS LOVE YOU

Words and Music by
DOLLY PARTON

128

will_ al - ways_ love_ you._____ I____

will_ al - ways_ love_ you._____

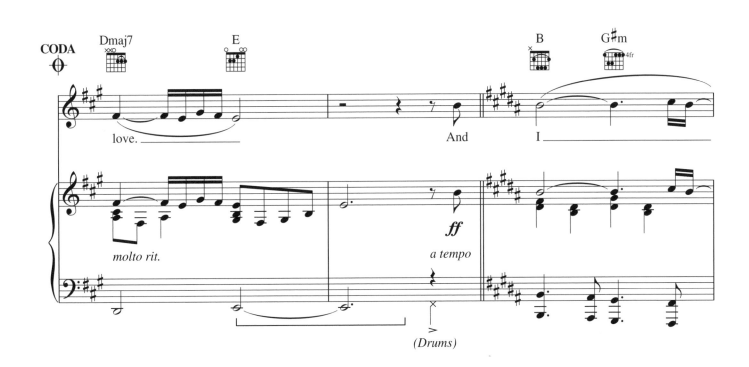

love._____   And   I_____

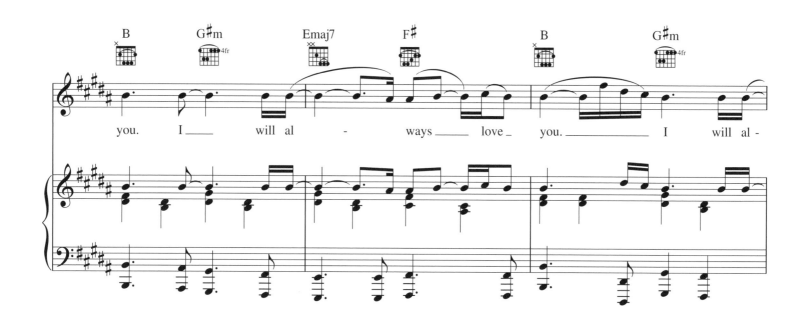

Additional Lyrics

3. I hope life treats you kind.
And I hope you have all you've dreamed of.
And I wish to you, joy and happiness.
But above all this, I wish you love.

IT'S TOO LATE

Words and Music by CAROLE KING
and TONI STERN

Stayed in bed all morn-in' just to pass the time. ___
used to be so eas-y, liv-in' here with you. ___

There's some-thin' wrong here, there can be no de-ny-in'. One of us ___ is chang-in', or
You were light and breez-y, an' I knew ___ just what to do. Now you look so un-hap-py, and I ___

may-be we've just ___ stopped try-in'. ___
___ feel ___ like a fool. ___

And it's too ___

JUST THE WAY YOU ARE

Words and Music by
BILLY JOEL

Don't go chang-ing _____ to try and please _ me. _____

You nev-er let me down _ be-fore. _____ Mm, _____ mm.

_____ Don't i-mag - ine _____ you're too fa-mil - iar.

KILLING ME SOFTLY WITH HIS SONG

Words by NORMAN GIMBEL
Music by CHARLES FOX

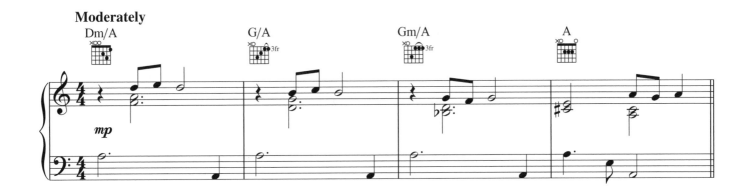

I heard _ he sang ___ a good _ song,
I felt ___ all flushed _ with fe - ver,
He sang _ as if _____ he knew _ me

I heard he had _
em - bar - rassed by _
in all my dark _

_ a style,
_ the crowd.
_ de - spair.

and so ___ I came ___ to see ___ him to
I felt _ he found _ my let - ters and
And then _ he looked _ right through _ me as

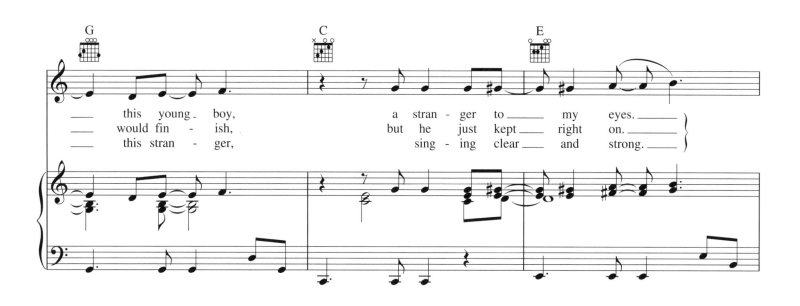

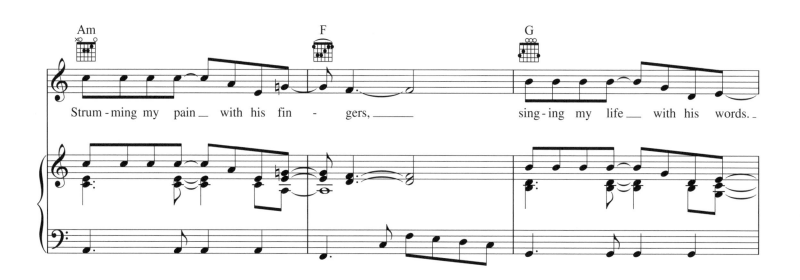

KISS FROM A ROSE

Words and Music by
SEAL

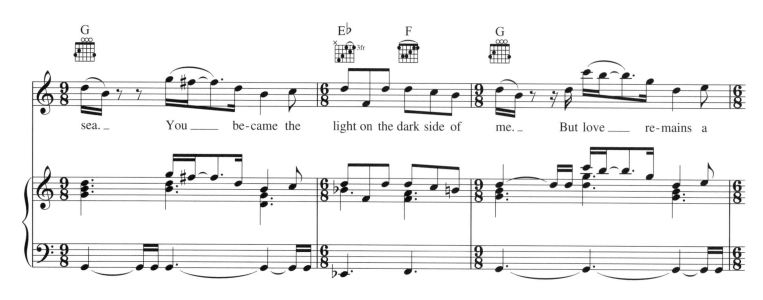

LOVE WILL KEEP US TOGETHER

Words and Music by NEIL SEDAKA
and HOWARD GREENFIELD

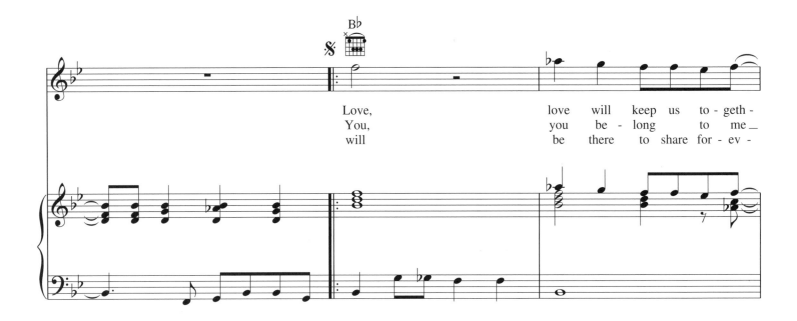

MACK THE KNIFE
from THE THREEPENNY OPERA

English Words by MARC BLITZSTEIN
Original German Words by BERT BRECHT
Music by KURT WEILL

Oh, the shark has _____ pret - ty teeth, dear, _____ and he shows them _____ pearl - y white. _____ Just a jack - knife _____ has Mac - heath, dear, _____ and he keeps it _____ out of

MOON RIVER

from the Paramount Picture BREAKFAST AT TIFFANY'S

Words by JOHNNY MERCER
Music by HENRY MANCINI

MRS. ROBINSON
from THE GRADUATE

Words and Music by
PAUL SIMON

Moderately Bright

And here's to you, ____ Mis-sus Rob - in - son, ____ Je - sus loves you more ____

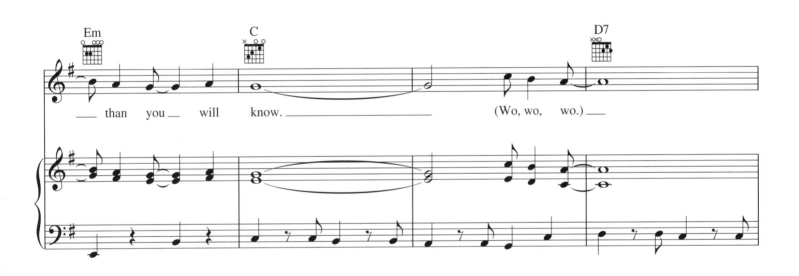

____ than you ____ will know. _____ (Wo, wo, wo.) ____

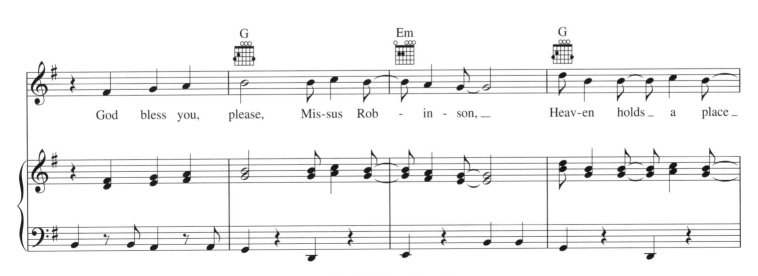

God bless you, please, Mis-sus Rob - in - son, ____ Heav-en holds ____ a place ____

MY HEART WILL GO ON

(Love Theme from 'Titanic')

from the Paramount and Twentieth Century Fox Motion Picture TITANIC

Music by JAMES HORNER
Lyric by WILL JENNINGS

NEED YOU NOW

Words and Music by HILLARY SCOTT,
CHARLES KELLEY, DAVE HAYWOOD
and JOSH KEAR

D.S. al Coda

noth - in' ___ at all. ___ It's a

CODA

I ___ just need __ you now. ___

NOT READY TO MAKE NICE

Words and Music by DAN WILSON,
EMILY ROBISON, MARTIE MAGUIRE
and NATALIE MAINES

* *Recorded a half step lower.*

ROLLING IN THE DEEP

Words and Music by ADELE ADKINS
and PAUL EPWORTH

PLEASE READ THE LETTER

Words and Music by ROBERT PLANT,
JIMMY PAGE, MICHAEL PEARSON
and STEPHEN JONES

cra - zy how __ it all __ turned out, __ we need-ed so __ much more. __

Please read the let - ter that I wrote. __

Please read the let-ter that I wrote. __ *Instrumental ad lib.*

Repeat ad lib. and Fade

REHAB

Words and Music by
AMY WINEHOUSE

Retro Blues

They tried to make me go to re - hab, __ I __ said, __ "No, __ no, __ no."

Yes, __ I been __ black, but when __ I come __ back, you won't

know, __ know, __ know. __ I ain't got the time, __

and if my dad - dy ___ thinks ___ I'm fine, _____ he's

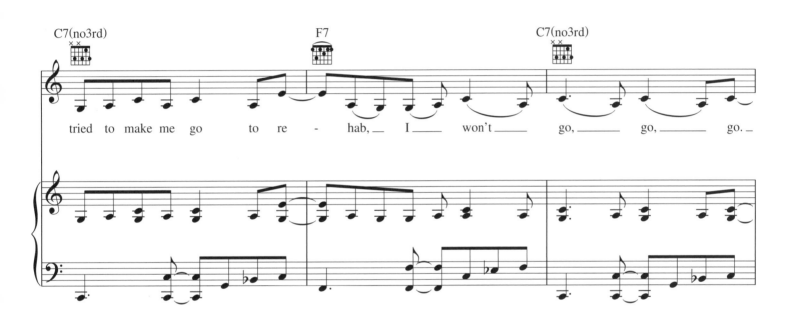

tried to make me go to re - hab, __ I ___ won't ___ go, ___ go, ___ go. __

I'd rath - er be at home _____
The man said, "Why you think _____
I won't ev - er want to ___ drink _____

ROSANNA

Words and Music by
DAVID PAICH

SAILING

Words and Music by
CHRISTOPHER CROSS

SMOOTH

Words by ROB THOMAS
Music by ROB THOMAS and ITAAL SHUR

Medium Latin Rock

Man, it's a hot one.
one thing,

Like sev - en inch - es from the mid - day sun. ___ Well, I hear your whis - per and the

if you would leave it'd be a cry - ing shame. ___ In ev - 'ry breath and ev - 'ry

STRANGERS IN THE NIGHT
adapted from A MAN COULD GET KILLED

Words by CHARLES SINGLETON and EDDIE SNYDER
Music by BERT KAEMPFERT

(Theme From)
A SUMMER PLACE
from A SUMMER PLACE

Words by MACK DISCANT
Music by MAX STEINER

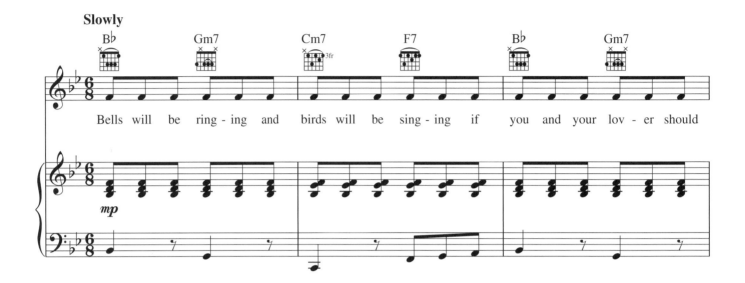

Bells will be ring-ing and birds will be sing-ing if you and your lov-er should

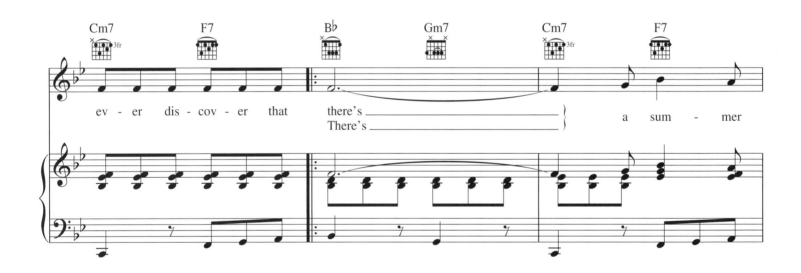

ev-er dis-cov-er that there's _____
There's _____
a sum-mer

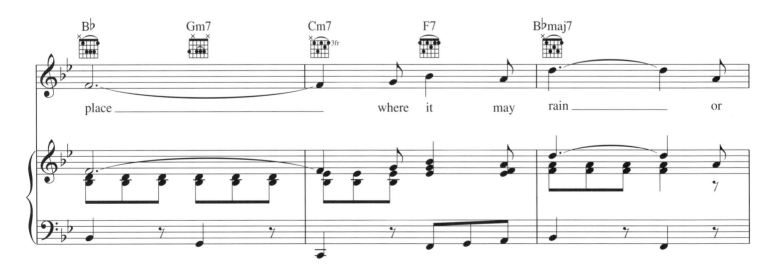

place _____ where it may rain _____ or

SUNNY CAME HOME

Words and Music by SHAWN COLVIN
and JOHN LEVENTHAL

Sun-ny came home to her fa-v'rite room. _ Sun-ny sat down in the

A TASTE OF HONEY

Words by RIC MARLOW
Music by BOBBY SCOTT

Moderately slow

Winds may blow o'er the ic - y sea, ___ I'll
leave be - hind my ___ heart to wear ___ and
ne'er came back to his love so fair ___ and

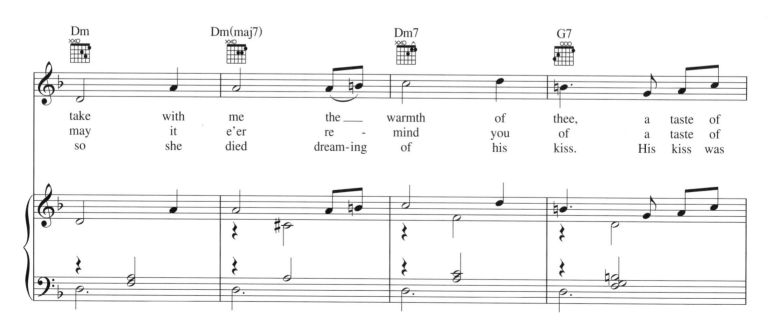

take with me the ___ warmth of thee, a taste of
may it e'er re - mind you of a taste of
so she died dream-ing of his kiss. His kiss was

246

TEARS IN HEAVEN

Words and Music by ERIC CLAPTON
and WILL JENNINGS

Be - yond the door ___ there's peace, I'm sure, __

THIS MASQUERADE

Words and Music by
LEON RUSSELL

*Guitar solo sounds an octave lower than written.

UNFORGETTABLE

Words and Music by
IRVING GORDON

UP, UP AND AWAY

Words and Music by
JIMMY WEBB

264

USE SOMEBODY

Words and Music by CALEB FOLLOWILL, NATHAN FOLLOWILL,
JARED FOLLOWILL and MATTHEW FOLLOWILL

Syncopated Rock

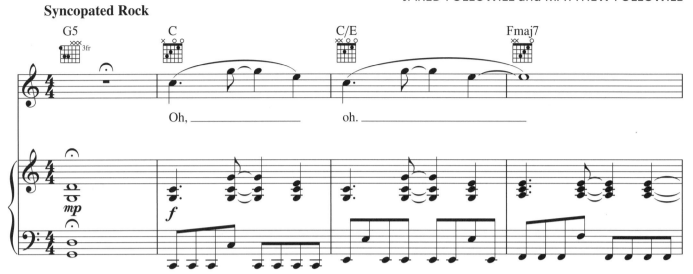

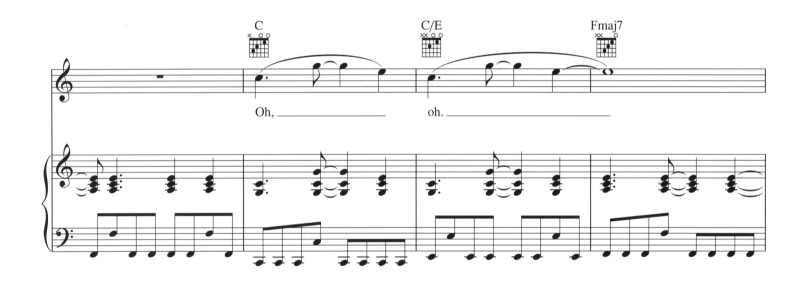

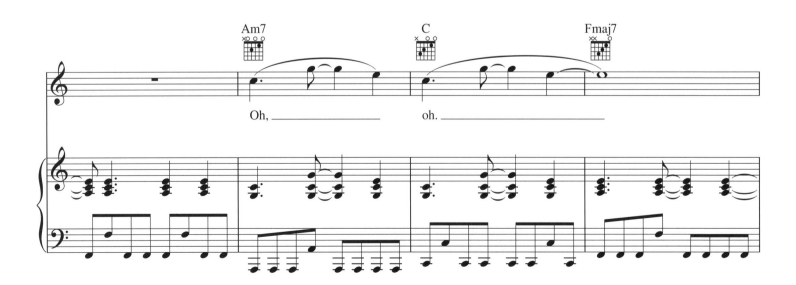

VOLARE
(Nel blu, dipinto di blu)

Music by DOMENICO MODUGNO
Original Italian Text by D. MODUGNO and F. MIGLIACCI
English Lyric by MITCHELL PARISH

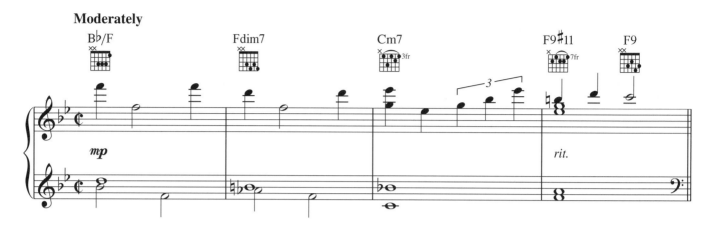

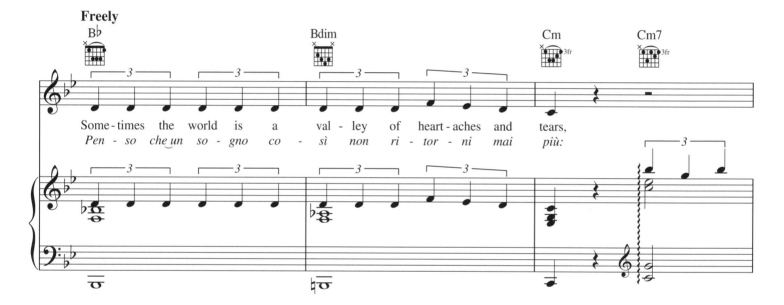

Some-times the world is a val-ley of heart-aches and tears,
Pen - so che un so - gno co - sì non ri - tor - ni mai più:

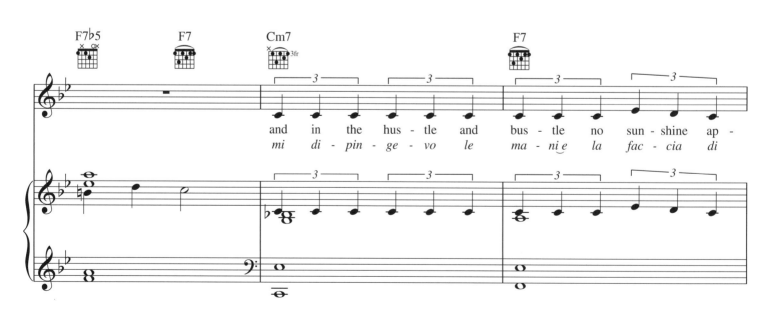

and in the hus-tle and bus-tle no sun-shine ap-
mi di - pin - ge - vo le ma - ni e la fac - cia di

oh! _____
oh! _____
No won-der my hap-py heart sings, your
nel blu, __ di - pin - to di blu, fe -

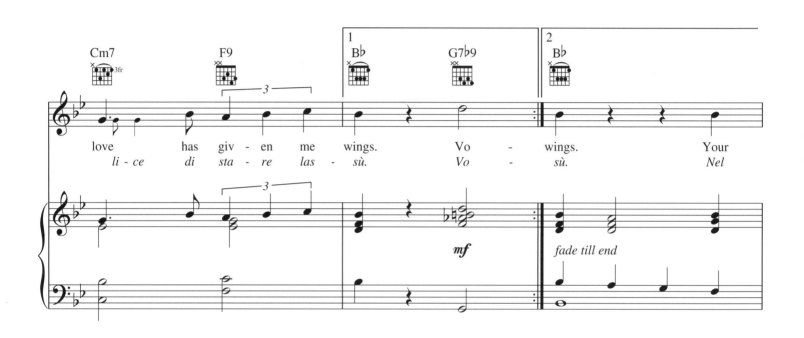

love has giv - en me wings. Vo - wings. Your
li - ce di sta - re las - sù. Vo - sù. Nel

love has giv - en me wings. Your love has giv - en me wings.
blu, di - pin - to di blu, fe - li - ce di sta - re las - sù.

WHAT'S LOVE GOT TO DO WITH IT

Words and Music by TERRY BRITTEN
and GRAHAM LYLE

Slow Rock

You must un - der - stand, _ though the touch of _ your hand _ makes my
may seem _ to you _ that I'm act - ing _ con - fused _ when you're

pulse re - act, _
close to _ me. _

that it's on - ly _ the thrill _ of
If I tend to _ look dazed, _ I

boy meet - ing girl, _ op - po - sites at - tract. _
read it _ some - place, _ I got cause to _ be. _

It's
There's a

WALK ON

Music by U2
Lyrics by BONO
Dedicated to AUNG SAN SUU KYI

And I know ___ it aches, ___ and your heart, it breaks. ___ You can on-ly take ___ so much. _____ Walk _____ on. _____

Additional Lyrics

All that you reason,
Each lonely time, all that I'm feelin' in my mind,
All that you sense,
All that you scheme,
All you dress up and
All that you seem.
All you create,
All that you wreck,
All that you hate...

WE ARE THE WORLD

Words and Music by LIONEL RICHIE
and MICHAEL JACKSON

WHAT A FOOL BELIEVES

Words and Music by MICHAEL McDONALD
and KENNY LOGGINS

* Recorded a half step higher.

THE WIND BENEATH MY WINGS

from the Original Motion Picture BEACHES

Words and Music by
LARRY HENLEY and JEFF SILBAR